THE MEDIUM

BOOKS BY THEODORE WEISS

Selections from *The Note-Books
of Gerard Manley Hopkins*

THE CATCH *(Poems, 1951)*

OUTLANDERS *(Poems, 1960)*

GUNSIGHT *(A Long Poem, 1962)*

THE MEDIUM *(Poems, 1965)*

THE
MEDIUM

POEMS BY

THEODORE WEISS

———

THE MACMILLAN COMPANY · NEW YORK

COLLIER-MACMILLAN LIMITED · LONDON

Some of the poems in this book first appeared in the following publications: *The Beloit Poetry Journal, Chelsea, Epoch, The Fat Abbot, MSS, The Nation, The New Republic, Quartet, Saturday Review, The Sewanee Review, The Yale Literary Magazine,* and *The Yale Review.* "In the Round," "Reapings," "The Web," and "Through the Strings" were first published in *Poetry.*

First Printing

The Macmillan Company, New York
Collier-Macmillan Canada Ltd., Toronto, Ontario
Library of Congress catalog number: 65-20168
Printed in the United States of America

For Renée

CONTENTS

THE MEDIUM 1

Thursday on the Ark

PARADIS PERDU 5

IN THE ROUND 9

WHITE ELEPHANTS 11

A MEDITATION 14

A WORLD TO DO 16

THE REAPINGS 18

THE LATEST WORD 19

AS I FORGET 21

A COVENANT 23

INSIDE 24

THE MORAL 26

A Satyr's Hide

INTO SUMMER 29

THROUGH THE STRINGS 31

OUT OF YOUR HANDS 36

THE WEB 40

ON STUFFING A GOOSE 42

LIZZIE HARRIS 44

A DAB OF COLOR 46

CATER-COUSINS 47

BY DESIGN 49

TWO FOR HEINRICH BLEUCHER 50

Airs for Caliban

A COMPETITION 61

CLOTHES MAKETH THE MAN 63

IN ANY CASE 65

STUDYING FRENCH 67

RUINS FOR THESE TIMES 69

AN OPENING FIELD 72

SONG TOWARD MORNING 75

FOR HOPKINS AT OXFORD 78

THE VISIT 79

THE MEDIUM

Fog puffed from crusted snow, rain sputters
midnight over them. Her words, a kind
of browsing in themselves, rise, cloud-bound,
by him in the bed.
                  She says, "I know
now why I have no memory. It's come to me,
a revelation. I must keep my thinking
open; I am not, like others, scribbled
all over by whatever happens."
                          He answers,
"Revelation? That's what you've always been
to me; by way of you have I not slithered
under the skin of things?"
                      "Cleansed of words,
my fears and doubts cast off, the fears
that words invent, I see each thing, free
at last to its own nature, see it free
to say exactly what it is."
                    "As for our primo-
genitor," he chimes in, "beside his twilit doorway, bent after the long day's chores
on the seraphic visit, meantime calling
things by their first name again."
                      "You won't
believe that people waken in my sleep
and like the moon, self-enlightened, speak
a language I don't know, move in a language
so itself one needn't know."
                      "Dreams,"
he nods, "do such things, like you attune
the dim as well as the emphatic phrases
I live in, the world become a bob-
bingly translucent globe, that round,
piped like Aeolus' impassioned winds

into a tiny bag,
              then popped, grape-
sweet, upon my tongue, for you beside me
sounding its fanfare. Such cornucopia
your lip and hand."
                  "How you do go on!
Unless you curb these peacock speeches you
love strutting in, how will you ever hear
another's words?
                Now listen to me. My father
lives again, in the special space I keep
for him here in my sleep, as he really is,
nothing but his fundamental voice,
directness daylight always must obscure,
cluttered as we are with long dead habits
and with failures, rage, my own and his,
encrusting us."
            The dream flushed on her still
addresses him through her without a sound:
"The time will come when your time comes;
the role meant for you slamming shut,
none of your wit, your artful dodgings,
able to hide you then, each thing you do
at last will prove effective, like a lion
grinding through your side."
                As moonlight
brims the fog, he hears, in books lined up
around them, richly scored, a honey pouring
through the words, the language passing
speakers, too imperious for words.

Thursday on the Ark

PARADIS PERDU

To cram one's mouth with other men
and hear the rattling of their spoons
in speech, to order wine that in the foam,
the evanescing of their oaths,
a hairy hand reach forth, cocksure
that apples, did they ripen into talk
of that maledicted day, would mutter so . . .

I

In a capital, for centuries
in fickle words itself,
yet new to us, we walked
the narrow, furtive streets
incognito as gods. To be
the middle of a world

    unseen,
            unheard!

                 Winter
full-blown in the wake
of nuns, gamins scurry in
and out, all secrets shared
in lingua franca of the wind,
rubbing up the naked trees.

Through the limbs we go
into a prickly privacy
and out to lovers bedded
in the park, rehearsing
April, fruit, and lark,
those by whom the story's

told: pupil Héloïse,
Blanche, the Lily Queen,

5

burning Joan, all passing
—a *bon jour, bon jour!*—
through the Arc de Triomphe
as Paris and his lady did.

II

And cosy as a pair
of clover-snuggled katydids,
we ate choice meals, drank
fervid wines, consorted with
a siren music * and, the gods
no more divine, made love

that incredible first week . . .
then the days fell dumb;
we rambled in a crumbling
tunnel of the endless length
of all the backward ages
of our ignorance: hoary

gullets cackling winds
for words, the winds blew
through each thing, blew
things back to a time
before their names; acts,
untaming, turned on us

till even the moon,
piling up its gritty banks
in our back room, was X.
O the stumbling icy miles
like Sanskrit swarming
under our noses. We were,

---

* A cabaret, celebrating in a series of acts famous books of poetry—*Les
Fleurs du Mal, E. A. Poë, Alcools,* etc., climaxed its show with an extrava-
ganza, a Gallic version of *Paradise Lost.*

III

there in Paris (our mouths
frozen crocks, mirror
stuck—odd faces staring
back—much like the dandy
on the wall, ever near
and ever near, yet never

touching his love), the inside-
out of the Puritans—unhappy
far-fetched comparison!
For there in a strange land,
horizons red, flamboyant
red, the fowl flying

bedizens only temptation
said, our forefathers
hoarded antique breath.
Believe! Red men, the dead
of winter, prophets, fuming,
come alive . . . terror-

nested, huddled one
against another like poor
blackbirds carrying through
the Great Frost, honoring
their losses, they survived.
Still the Word came down

and broke like flaky
crumbs east winds puffed
into turkeys ruffling, full-
mouthed plums. The twistings
hived the movements, good
morning, of God

                  cocking
His green thumb.

And O

the crowing under the rose-
bush: somehow children
in that creaky hot-house
under the long, stiff noses
got themselves composed . . .

This it is to mumble other men,
to wander through their lands and times
naming that you've never seen or done.
Yet spot the boats at rotted wharves,
unloading crates at night? Squint
for all you're worth: smuggled goods
from barbarous interiors hove into sight!

IN THE ROUND

Catching yourself, hands lathery
and face ajar, inside the glass,
you wryly smile; watching, you know
you're in for it:
                    and in the twinkle
of your eye the horny butting goat
and jutting horny bull, the weasel,
goose bedraggled and the wren
with greedy bill go flashing by;
there too, recoiled as from the shadow
of itself in a teetering pool, claws
contracted to one cry, the spider
crouches in its den.
                    What gusto
can it be that blows its violence
through a locust's violin, mad summer
burnishing in such midge mouths?

These the routine heroes, poised,
in resolution black as bulls,
deadlocked in a din of warriors
grappling centaurs—prizes near:
a heifer nibbling grass; the rouged
and gossamer girl, nothing diaphanous
as the fearful hope that flits,
a fire's touch, inside her breath,
each prize forgotten—on a vase.

One wonders how the clay withstands
not only time, but what such hands,
great hearts, command from one another,
art and earth, the audience amazed.

Still, though clay crack, necks
break, twitchy as a cock, they stand,
engrossed and going on, a Bach
of a beetle, strutting like a yokel,
nightlong at its tongs and bones.

WHITE ELEPHANTS

. . . and were these in the ark as well?

Alone except for one bowlegged, bounding
cur whose yipping scored the frozen world,
that afternoon we tracked the neighbor grounds,
two people and a dog in a sprawled estate.

The snow before and after, trees black above
it as below, had molded to the dips
and curvings of the ground. Winds too like drifts
folded round the stubble sticking through.
Beyond, the Catskills, blue under blue-honed sky,
humped, recumbent days on days forsaken.

Following the road-bend to the coach-house,
we sidled through its doors; there considered
its first inhabitants—their shiny flanks
and tails, their whinnyings and oaten smells—
could they be seen in oaken panelings,
hoofs clattering still upon the stony floor.

Out of it, we skirted the dirty mansion,
these several years fitfully alive, lurched
to one side for the weather's shifty weight,
its corniced cherubim and cedars, carved
in cedar, mostly shed.
                           The formal gardens
at their stiffest now, their fountain billowed,
snowbird struggling in its ice-jagged flight,
the Hudson just below had banked, a moonlight,
freezing while it fell, one rigor mortis.

As if fearing those the storm must satisfy
(the stone-pale woman in the alcove, arms
set round two children, and a dog beside,

caught in his friskiness as in their spell),
we went no nearer.
                            But winds struck us, fluster
at the pane of flakes off rubbing boughs.
Or was it blur of frantic beckonings,
now less than thistledown upon the blast,
a curtain flickering the moonlit-shoulder-
shadowed waltzes, glimpses of the Danube,
as from a time that closed with the passing
of the last great lady of the house?

It never closed:
                            cracks pried by children
and damp cellar kin, relentless for their chance,
the house shook, shook out its occupants
to quake again with merriment of those
for the first time enjoying total tenancy.

And O what marrying was there, what free-
for-all in mirror, spider, paired-off drapes;
the letters, scattered in a corner, wound up
with ants and wasps at capers, fern's sly mind.

The seed in itself after its own kind,
in each smuggled the deeds (stowed away
below as in the rafters' crevices
dragons, bats, pigweed) that grew the Garden
beyond itself, flowered above the Flood:

crimes, failures, flowering too, the first root
must have journeyed through to this, the cluster
it would become for not a few to carry,
smoky over purple as of some shy episode,
a rainbow tangled glistening in its foliage.

And still the rickety mansion stood; the little
dog, yipping round and round, snuffling out

huge tracks, lolloped over its racy, curving lawns
till the mountains swayed, a graceful, lurching,
trunk-entwining, cloud-behowdahed two by two.

The outgrounds rallying, the stallions that
once galloped here, cows nodding to their stalls,
the bugs and mice tucked in their cranny darks
like jewels gleaming in a mummied tomb,
all seemed to fly to a single joyous yoke.

And clouds for twilight flushed with riches.
Days on days swept in a rush, at once
the dirty snow went bright, those first tracks up
and down the dips and curvings of the air,
brown shoots off like till-now-drowsing crows,
the flake-doves off, no rest for their feet
beyond the stubble waking in their beaks.

A MEDITATION

I know, my love, that thought began
when woman—after her her man—
was sped from paradise. For earlier
it would have cramped the scene, super-
fluous as hats upon a pomegranate,
leaves to shade figleaves. But that's
what happens—thought—when we're apart
or when, though heart climb into heart,
distance like dusk upon a day creeps
into your eyes, the overwhelming sleep.

Now is not paradise, yet of its time
as you approach, the morning grown
lightheaded on your flame-tipt hair.
Not paradise, but ripplings in the air
of a metropolis nearby, its prospect
rounded out with light-bestippled smoke,
the bustle from the distance a patina
on the whole, set off by spires,
each pane of which like crowded fires
glares, the streets a daft careening

to the center where, a fountain hover-
ing, yet not delayed by what it over-
looks (absolved the complicated murder-
ings), a garden stakes the midday ardors,
rakish leaves and odors giving quarter.
Not paradise, my dear, but little matter
since I am Adam at myriad removes
and you a twilit Eve it best behooves
to meet me, stay me in my fitful rovings.
Thought, I must, alas, admit it, love,

even as I loathe it, one of my chief
loves. And though I wear it, grieving
sign of Cain, furrowing my brow
like one strained after joys glowing
distantly, you in this urgent city
you draw round me, rich in rage and pity,
license me to all the Adam I can
bear. In our time of man and woman,
whatever havoc spins along our streets,
I charge the center via every doubt.

A WORLD TO DO

for Jeffrey

"I busy too," the little boy
said, lost in his book
about a little boy, lost
in his book, with nothing

but a purple crayon
and his wits to get him out.
"Nobody can sit with me,
I have no room.
            I busy
too. So don't do any noise.
We don't want any noise
right now."
            He leafs
through once, leafs twice;
the pictures, mixed with windy
sighs, grow dizzy,
                  world
as difficult, high-drifting
as the two-day snow that can
not stop.
            How will the bushes,
sinking deeper and deeper,
trees and birds, wrapt
up, ever pop
              out again?
Any minute now the blizzard,
scared and wild, the animals
lost in it—O the fur,

the red-eyed claws, crying
for their home—may burst

into the room. Try words
he's almost learned
                        on them?
He sighs, "I need a man here;
I can't do all this work
alone."
            And still, as though
intent on reading its own
argument, winter continues
thumbing through itself.

THE REAPINGS

Firstlings of grief,
pain in all its sweetest fat
and dew, abounding in my sinews
its sinews, like a mettlesome, gay
youth . . .
                    years later,
the fields gone over a thousand
times, every flower spied on,
every weed, like a royal being,
golden foreigner,
                    as though
one, not seeing, might forget,
let loose its secret, the reality . . .
years later, the basic truths,
their seasons
                    in each season,
gone over and over, still grief
strikes, a new-forged arrow, finds
out fresh wounds, its resource,
surprising, relevant,
                    of pain.
The hands clutch themselves
in the wrestle; how learn
to let go like a nakedness in this
fluent fall,
                    a warbling rain?
And how be thankful, name
with love this one that seeks
me out, demands a stature of me,
a strength,
                    so arrogant for me,
I hardly knew I own? Breaking,
I lie there, threshed, before me,
gifts, the firstlings, weathered
on that flying stone.

THE LATEST WORD

As though a chaffinch
out of some faraway spring,
chirping its other-world patter
as it perches on the nearby bough,
revises via bare sprig, bole,
and root the whole commonwealth,
the language, all of it
alive, goes on;
                              his straggly beard
a fire-talking bush, a rabbi
hunches over you, thumbing through,
then concentrating on a passage
understandably obscure.
                              His village,
in its local seasons and occasions
collaborating with the stroller
seasons as they hold forth, throws
curious, kind light on the black-
and-white until,
                              his absentminded
drone a tantalizing promise
in your ear (thick flocks perhaps,
their pre-dawn maple-chittering
the rudiments of music making
in the air),
                              the stiff lines,
crackling, blaze like branches
(the village, fled in flames,
regained the glimpse of paradise
lost, in cries, floating heaven-
ward, the soot of flesh and terror,
then settled into roots and out
in leaves, thoughts, flowering).

A new word sounds, so meant
for you both, so loose, so taut
through your body, you cannot tell
one from the other, two at least
caught in one breath.

AS I FORGET

for David Schubert (1913–1946)

I rummaged for that thought again,
that feeling and that image where,
as it burst forth, my life began.

The dead, I said, whatever we do,
alone can tell us that we have
to learn: precisely as they owe

what life they now enjoy to us,
in turning to them we must grow
the more alive and thereby blessed,

their wisdom gathering on us. Sure
of it, I tried to struggle back.
But fighting every clever pleasure

of forgetting hemmed the way,
I soon despaired of meeting him
who might have told me, passing day,

how to withstand these temptings and
deceits by how much he had paid.
I soon despaired, my groping hand

huge with emptiness. And then
I said, Is only loss, its strength
ransacking all, one steady dun,

the thing I have to learn, and there
that image, feeling, thought embraces
me with grave and finished air?

Though pansies, lionhearted scholars,
ponder sorrow, in his words,
they utter gaiety and splendor.

Of blooms a girl the mignonette
engrossing me, I have him, am him,
and most of all, as I forget.

A COVENANT

You, walking up the path before me,
wonder aloud what it feels like
to grow much older, wonder whether
you will be where I, ten years
ahead (or is it ten behind?), now am.
With your head bent sideways
you remind me of a former friend
as though, two decades dead,
he suddenly stepped forth to find me
out again, this time a little differently.

Now, when it seemed the ark
was finished, all the passengers in,
so too the animals belonged to it,
the home quay out of sight, you
appear with her, a sort of window
opened on a new-lit, eager view.
The land I long ago forgot, shrugged
off like a childish story, starts
up, more fabulous than ever.

This you do, she beside you,
with the copiously touching gifts
you bring in brimming hands and eyes
of helplessness, a youth you've not
yet reached the bitter end of.
Your love, your desire to get it
all said, comes out sometimes sullen,
sometimes curt and quarrelsome,
for the attention it can never get
enough of.
            And the bugs and beasts
I thought completed pair religiously
as ever; to the dove as to the raven
wrangling, snarling still give ground.

INSIDE

Despite your battering doubts,
my friend, the tallest walls are down,
down though people turn on you,
blind, insurmountable stone backs
that block you from the town
in which, you say, your triumph lies,
and, far within, that upright room,
superior to eyes, shrining the homecome idols of your dream.
                              Like Lot
no doubt, that scrawny one in courage
and yet brave, you are doubly out:
first, for yourself, then even more—
as though to fathom distances
in strangeness you would not dare
alone—for the beings you can see
the others, raucous, let be only
as they can belittle them, invisible,
for the titillations of their senses.

Still, I repeat, as rowdy horns
go blasting round beyond the fences
and defenses of your delicate though
sounder pipe—you desperately knowing
your two small children, a first wife
and parents as well, the sacrifices
to the ruthless wings that rustle
through your blood—the walls are down,
not only for your terrible frail will,
this stubborn folly you persist in,

music you must serve, but for
our friendship, growing as the traffic
swerves from side to side, a music

loud and steady, bronzen to abide,
and in the love you know for her
that batters through your ablest fear
and batters down your sky-eclipsing
pride. Better say that by this warmth,
the blasts according of your breaths,
you open up the town again, inside.

THE MORAL

The dark figures, lunged ahead,
out of their twisted lust for heaven
and the stars, into the sea, into the dirt,
your father, mine, and that benighted
company,
            aeries predatory birds
grow sleek in, their lives crackling
like holocausts, the concentration camps
where tortures, working out hell's
ideology, excel,
               those, sounding
through our minds like bells, ringing us
into the catacombs that man can be,
shall they also light us, lead
us through the midnight
                  of our days?
We have warmed our hands at many strange
fires, many stray. The summer's jew's-
harp has twanged out hot blues
of some superior pain,
               its fireflies
faraway torches for a pilgrimage
to altars crammed with sacrifices. Cries,
backs bent, glistening in bloody sweat,
to accurate, gay lashes,
             the shriek,
a phosphorescence sizzling, of the mouse,
accomplished in the likely clutches
of the hawk, like lilies in a paradigm
spell out the moral
             of our tale.
Whatever has happened, diverse ravishings
that love to bask in balmy weather
of a scream, the passionate failures,
the perfect despairs, these never fail us.

A Satyr's Hide

INTO SUMMER

Some days ago, to stop the leaping
weeds, on both sides of the path
workmen scorched these fields.
A short time after, as he passed
the charcoal-velvety, zigzag tracks,
he smelt the strange blend of the
burnt and the growing.
                              But now,
just over the black, something flags,
green flicked here and there,
but mostly a transparent papery
brown, like stubborn ghosts caught
in the fire and yet come through,
nodding as though to say, "This is
as much as we can do."
                              And he who
tried to pierce the classroom tedium,
to move his students to a grove,
a clearing where the green remains,
recalls some struggled into words,
then fallen back, eyes flickering
a second as though caught with sun.

And they, like one's best hopes
and feelings, singed yet wrangling
through, knowing nothing but the need
to go on, into summer?
                              Soon,
of their own greed and by the tangle
of numbers, the weeds will do
what the greasy fire was meant to.

But now each must heed the music
mumbling in him—in some crazy way,

on top of the brown, green sticks out,
and a whitish, tiny kind of flower—
that strange blend of the burnt
and the growing.

THROUGH THE STRINGS

I

To be free of the fingers,
the need to be making,
to be slaking the moon
under the tongue:
                        to be free
of the feelings that weave,
siren, savage, adder-like
striking, through the lyre.

Again and again, gasped
in the seethe of its leaves,
August requires breath;
November, strident, chafes
at my tuning.
                        Let rains—
the lightnings nestled
by their coil—ride, cradled
in clouds; let winds, tree-
modulated, nod.

II

                        But now
the lightfoot season, slid
through metal and the lidded
seed,
            my lyre like dead wood
taken, greedily confronts
with the stare of the thing
called five petals.

III

        To be free
of the fingers—why should she,
gone, except as she cries out
in me, seeking some body, be
a wedding of winter and summer
so singly?

        Through the rock-
ribbed earth she draws me,
gentian, twilit here, elsewhere
for the somber lights passed
through—

        the fingers once
love- and passion-clever, moans
dirt-stuffed, with glances sealed
into the root—

        guttering smoky,
cloven faces . . .

        so singly
as though the flower of the long
tongue in fruition's final outrage
uttered the one unerring word.

IV

Long and long I have stormed
through the strings, the wrangle
under the breath, the Dog toothing
ravenous heads in the groin.

She gone at the turning,
the others, charmed, let loose,
ensnarled in my song, stay with me,
clamoring for more.

        Too long
I lie, too long in this slow river-
bed the leaves make, huddled
dead sighs.

V

Last smiting of strings

(shades, responsive again—
                        dense
verdure, risen undertow, of listening
cypresses, apt pitch-pines, river-
rapt willows—
                        my loyal convoy,
a match for the dark, shall I not
bring her back?):
                        bunched notes
plucked, petal by petal, a resonant
curve throbs through my fingers:

leaped above the sprung bar,
gaze, and gazing breast, thigh
glistening:
                        one tentative step, tripped
falling, fallen, far beyond that
viper spite, her disappearing
surpasses my speediest cry;
                                    but there,
there, in that white a loitering . . .

VI

try catching it, no watery moonlight
more elusive.
                        The motes have gone
out, like echoes, the notes, of a cry—
mine? hers?—in mockery.
                                    And nothing
more than racketing chats, flicker
like eyelids of sparrows, low
to the ground, oaks also forsaking,
poplars in droves?

VII

          Fingers, writhing,
fang themselves; the feelings trample,
mountainous. How bear such pitch
of yearning,
          this strange hand
upon the lyre, strums by mine, strums
through, now strums—a storm begins
to stir in me—alone?
          Grown, grown
with every breath, the notes backfire,
buffet heart. (This covey after her,
did that twanging bring them?)
          Drop
me, lyre, drop. And play as you will
in spiders' tautened nets, the aspens
saying you, unfettered winds.
          Play
through the women, fury-bitten,
dammed by me. Let them, cries brimmed
to howls, attack.
          Like the gentian
under this rock, flying me free,
sticks, clods, deft hands at me, I am
plucked.

VIII

          Surely I rejoin her
whose love brought harmony
I did not need to play,
brought peace
          past savage night,
highnoon, a sweet extinction
of all fear, all longing,
till all loss began.
          Extinction
now must grant me peace again,

34

her face above, so fitting
then I thought it
                    my own
doing only, birds too, flowers,
out of singing, summer-breed-
ing tunes.

IX

            Breath quicker than wind,
I glide through the arching gate
of their stones,
                    down the route
ripped petals make upon the spurting
stream, into the grass, ground
opening.
            That one word going
under, earth's tide, the white
flower—
            see! the round sigh
of her (torches splutter behind,
the cloven faces), hand's last wave,
sky clutched in her hand—
                              surges
over, filling the mouth . . .

X

                    he, never
again looking past that shoulder,
reins in the hands of a will
that brooks no consent.

OUT OF YOUR HANDS

(on receiving W. C. Williams'
"Theocritus", June 5, 1953)

Though you regret it,
out of your hands it must go,
out of your hands still warm on it,
loving with the best love, a bare mind,
undaunted inside the hands, casting
the familiar line, a child fished,

a poem—the issue
life: this manuscript your note
calls "a unique copy" you would hate
to lose. How unique only those who try
to make as well, having staked out
their pleasurable awareness

in the clearing
of your verse, can know. June
now, the first sultry day, swept in,
one swollen glare, on the back of last
night's thundrous rain, the morning
looking as though its masons

just broke off.
And you, returning whence you
came, closer daily, have mailed us
your translation of Theocritus: *Idyl I*
after your local hundreds, ground
from which this new-fangled

garden of America
you still prune, hard as it is
to believe, has sprung. You return;
in age you relish that hungering again,

the virgin green—this a field
where crops nourish crops—

growing through
practiced hands. No yokel you
to luten notes, whatever disguise,
and of that few equipped to face Priapus
equally with old Chronos, grazing
in your tunes. You alone,

shepherd of cool
shades, beneath squat weeds
and runty twigs, refining silence,
manage among shrill horns to keep song
going, freshets as of a deep-down
source, that Pan, chase-worn,

exasperation only
reedy at his nostrils, find
a cove where revelry, love and folly
know some ease. Despite your vigilance
the gifts come to you hardly goat,
shag-white, or firstling kid,

a delicate fleshed
for being eaten before its milk
begins, you feed on bramble-berries,
make iron, refuse, yield. They no less—
hands not letting go except they,
naming, bless—must slip away.

Your poems, worked
like the cup, dipped in living
waters, given Thyrsis for his song,
will stay. These poems, passed through
whatever hands, mouths, will keep
the markings of your clean-

edged knife,
your voice informing them.
A seasoned breath poured in, sly
winds, involved in curving ivy, carved,
flickering through yellow flowers,
flaunt their airs: April, May,

frisky months again,
leading groves in frolic; ale-
wives, flashing tails in this sea-
dark surge; bees, drunken as in a mazy
rose—and all garlanding a girl,
in turn a mazy rose,

a ritual composed,
for her, fairer than the gods
might dream, your mind's familiar.
Beside this rouse a furrowed fisherman
on a furrowed rock, mending nets,
splicing knots, repairing

tangled lines and
lending skill to rods and pipes
that these release their wood's chief
ingrained spell. One pair of hands
to do all things, strike human
moods from time, a harmony

past need that makes
the need the more. Set to cast
now, the thousandth time—his whole
heart in it—the mighty net. And near
the veteran, straddling the ruddy
vineyard wall, indifferent

to grape-roused foxes,
winter, and the Foe, greedily

fixed at his foot, a boy, plaiting
star-flower stalks around short reeds
for a pet-cricket cage in intent,
wise and thoughtless joy.

THE WEB

for Hannah Arendt

High summer's sheen upon all things
that dust is glazed and I am lost
within the florid scene, I think
of someone stitched into a complex
tapestry; and sitting in a niche—
five glittering crows a crown
about her head, held there no doubt
by thread run through their feet,
but held as well, or so it seems,
by what she does and what she sings—
she stitches too,

                as one should sing,
absorbed by what she hears, so sing
the more, her glance, entwining
in her work, lit up, that radiance,
high summer's sheen, be visible
and piling in a telltale foam
from her shy skill, that all things
eagerly like stars around the moon
attain their story, listen to it,
from her lip and hand, her settled
will; and still, as she is nested
in her craft, like dolphins leaped
above their element, she spins.

Ah, let this be a lasting omen:
the world a moment takes its blessing
from the sleight-of-hand of woman,
and by our passion held in common,
as we when we were young, our limbs
air-borne, bore leaves and ballads
of the birds, the clouds and storms

and all the world beside mere flowering of our singled sigh;

                        thought
nothing of the skulking, not yet
lowering gloom such opulence must
shed; nor thought a wind, until now
banked or spent among our breath
with our consent, a gleaming shade
in our design, would, blowing,
blast the web—torn also by the tatter
crows, fled far beyond their thread-
bare wings—and, last, its instruments.

ON STUFFING A GOOSE

(after overhearing some students talk
knowingly of D. H. Lawrence)

Is this fame then and what it is to be
really alive, to go on living after flesh,
having failed, has been officially
hauled away?
       To cast a moment's spell
upon some distant man and girl, a feeling
of familiarity in a gust of fragrance
in a summer's night,
                of loneliness
made roomier as they recall his anguish,
as though flesh alone, one time and place,
one wife, a single set
                  of friends
were too confining and that life must be
let out to mine its basic cadence finally
in our pondering of it,
                  free of any
obligation save the pleasure that we take
in it. . . . My father was a great hand
at stuffing geese.
            In the cellar dark
he'd keep one penned. Knees grappling it,
he'd ram a special mash with dippers
of water down its throat.
                In time
that crate began to bulge; past waddling,
goose managed only belchy squawks.
We knew it ready.
             Somewhere in all this
I have a sense of what it is to be really
alive. Somewhere in the celebration

of that goose,
                    throned on a shiny
platter, for its mellow crackling skin
a jovial martyr, piping savors of a life
well lived,
                    our heart's gladness
in the occasion of picking the juicy meat
from the sides and the bones, in that
and remembering the sense abides.

LIZZIE HARRIS

First a rabbit died,
and then a crow.
The children knew they had
to go the measured way
of funeral.
But Whimpy
got the rabbit first;
without the creaky comfort
of a hearse he popped it
into kingdom-come.

So crow was left to find
its lasting room and board.

The weed-lost graveyard
just behind his house
a likely spot,
the oldest boy picked out
what seemed least occupied
the longest time, a plot
most fitting for a crow.

The name upon its pocky
stone was "Lizzie Harris."

Then banging on a pot
to beat the band, he led
a four-man funeral
to cries of "Good-bye,
Lizzie Harris, good-bye!"
as the youngest, dragging
Lizzie by the neck, brought
up the rear.

But Whimpy,
having sped one parted
guest, stayed home, intent
upon the welcome-mat,
to pay his full respects.

And so, unruffled, Lizzie
found her final nest.

A DAB OF COLOR

for R E

By dint of color
in his skin
that nature, unrelenting
innovator, dabbled in
(it marked him

off better than fences
can) a wind began,
a winter that companion-
ately and forever
went with him.
                O never
twit the artist, never
call him ivory-tower
scholar, bent
on anything but sense.

He knows—for he has
learned from nature—
that a little dab
of color, aptly mixed,
makes all the difference.

CATER-COUSINS

Having roused my feelings
to their utmost skills, with one
the other's prompter till they swelled
into a concert that revealed me, ringing,
past the self of knowing,
                              I wonder
now where they exert their wills
and where they tarry. For they are—
and I would be their truthful telling—
my one compelling story.
                              I wander
like a fugitive inside a scuffling crowd
or like this chilblained morning, blue
and mooning at the barred-in window,
dreaming of a long-
                              starved sun
(for only appetite can whet that eye
to light on such hunched, grizzly garden),
a show of passion. Let a blizzard
crack its frozen chaps,
                              Oh let
the scraps go flying in a fake event
that I forget this pallor and this emptiness by what distraction. A panic
in the streets,
                              bloody riotings
fire enjoys, disaster, mean more surely
than the days in their parade, anonymous
as glarings—whited, stone-blind eyes—
of statues.
                              Waiting may last
longer than we are, like calendars
thumbed to the end, then swept, dead

leaves, away? Ah, no. Those cater-
cousins
        having once been roused,
I, the roused in turn and deeply learned
in their lore, can answer—all the rest
cheap whores, indifferent, so costly—
though it be forever, to no other.

BY DESIGN

As one leaf borrows
fire from another, together
shining as they writhe like martyrs
wreathing in a larger truth,

so one face flared
and crackled in this anger,
then another. Day was never better
banked in airy fat forsythia,

fused as it swelled,
like metal heated, molding
in its run. Sun, petaled out, held
them till this later time,

and one leaf catches
fire from another, twirls
in all the crying antics of desire
that design alone is seen,

then not a single
lineament. Yet one face,
fiercely as I strained to pluck it
from its perch, remained

untouchable.
But now, the long day's
darkness over, that hid one,
and quite unbidden, startles forth;

in it, for it,
fire, banked and rid
of fever, moves like morning,
comfort to the night-racked forest.

TWO FOR HEINRICH BLEUCHER

A Satyr's Hide

I

In smoky light the students gawk
at pluming, reeled off from their lips,
as the speaker, groping, breaks
through words into some other air.

But one, apart, till now squinting
through the fumes he tries to fan
with a heavy lilac cluster, jeers:
"I am not difficult enough, not
like these by apathy alluring him.

He thinks persuasion can convert
them into peers, their dust at last
alive as though, stirred, the gods
were laboring within.
      And see
the grown-up men he hobnobs with,
artists fuddled as their paints,
perverts, crackpots, moldy peddlers
of ideas.
    Nobility gleaned from swamps!"

II

To see the divine matters, the stars that,
foiled by some events and fouled by others—
wars and trials and deaths—serenely shine . . .

one, old, bald, mottled, with a flattened beak,
bulbous as a growth under a toadstool,
in dress a bumpkin, barefoot in some kind

of fit ("not the sign of contemplation?"),
and in the middle of battle, onelegged, day-
long standing like a crane.
                           Or, chortling away,
joining ragged kids at hopscotch ("who's
to say wisdom itself, shirt bunched round
its spindly shanks, was not skipping too");

one with striplings, especially the handsome,
in any wretched tavern, rattling up his heels
the whole night through, relentless, prodding them
("beyond themselves, in chase perhaps of something only glimpsed, driving joy").

And then, cock crowing, nothing more to do
than watch the boats bustling at the wharves,
the bales and slaves ("spices like nodding winds
aroused, with distant names and places puffed
from sails. Athens travel enough: do not
the stars each night arrive, the famous gods,
incognito?").
                           Unfit for public office,
jester, gibing, bitter toward his superiors,
in court and out, with lingo, slops from
gutters still fresh on it, flaying alive.

Spellbinder too, throwing all who care to hear
into confusion and dismay as though
to say their lives are nothing but a slave's
("for the difficulties over which they, failing
to see through, toil, turmoil themselves"),
so making it impossible for some
to go on as they were.
                           A man to be trusted?
Little more than the lover he played along with,
drunk ("who ever saw him, wine unmixed,
goblet on goblet flashing like his wit,
inebriate?"), in very drunkenness

("of love") proclaiming him a grotesque, Silenus,
preceptor of mad Dionysus.
                              ("Remember
what those curious figures stowed: musk
like fragrances deep-wooded, weathered leaves
keep, caperings among the fauns and dryads,
deities at their numerous delights.")

That favorite pupil, crowned with violets,
bright ribbons dangling, wayward under splendor
like a fire, sprung full-panoplied
from the master's head and thigh ("full-panoplied,
as he himself admitted, had he heeded
that voice reclaiming him to his best nature
he forever fled"), with other young bloods
launched on matters so divine, might tread
down Athens, shiny pebble in his reeling.

("Might indeed: sealed off as he was,
his beauty dazzling, only havoc fed him,
deadly respite from his golden curse.
But the other without the State, he knew,
and the lovely haven, sovereign polis,
of its language, would be worse than dead.")

The old one—imagine it, death just ahead,
eternity approaching ("a sense of time
for everything")—amused himself by taking
for the first time in his life to verse-making
and the flute: ("a Paean to Apollo")
and fables, appropriately, out of Aesop!

A satyr play ("the true philosophy");
so cast him, judged by some the loftiest crag
in cloud-capped—temples like clouds; roads, markets,
rumbling with beauty—fastidious Athens.

"Never forget he did not have that hide
for nothing; shaggy capering, the goat-dance,
rooted him wherever, the course he followed
on the flute.
        Risk it was no doubt, a star
standing out in the open and confidently
twirling about itself, risk or that real thing
sometimes called folly, notes laureling his head;
yet earthiness and the mystery therefrom
never left him a moment:
                divine matters."

III

The lilac spray, plucked from one
peak of late spring, resilient still
as the words move through it, seems
to tingle in his hand.
        A deep lilac
breath, the speech in it the air
for ancient voices, rising, rousing
coupled shapes, he sees what man
might be,
        man finding out his place
within the frieze, a marble, breathing
heroes, gods, and satyrs, creatures
confident in flight.
        And in the drift
of words he lets the cluster sway,
its top clump heaviest for buds
closest together,
        still unopened
as though the life in the lilac
had surged through this stem
and on the way, tarrying,
        burst
into flower, then sped to the top,
but cut off before it could gather,

hung there,
                nubbly grapes or the plume
of a boy smitten in his first encounter.
Purpler they than the lavender open.
Yet the words soaring, he half expects
these last buds to respond.
                But death
always more on them, like lids that,
nearly lifted, now certainly would
not, he watches the lilac following
the laws, the scent gradually waning,
the head drooping.
                And when the speaker
stops, he offers it to him:
"If you will take it; I have had it
this hour."
                That one, flourishing it,
"The gift, you told me once, depends
on the receiver."
                On the receiver,
but also on the giver who,
in that delicious hunger of giving,
the last, the loveliest, loftiest love
of all, the light and scent of a self-
rewarding joy—gives with no notion
of reply.

The Wine-Skin Foot

Loose not the wine-skin foot, thou chief of men,
Until to Athens thou art come again.
Oracle of Delphi

. . . a rolling stone . . .

I

The wine-skin foot?
Well as one can he hides it, hid it most
when the land where he first found it
turned into a howling wilderness.

A growing wolf howl, steady twister, blew
through Berlin into Paris. And he saw it—
tyranny, what he loved crushed by the treason
of the state, at last full-blown, bloody—
countless death to stay.
                    (Did not his gentle
friend, to save his son from bestial-
ity and worse, kill him.) Words and deeds
there were, the gods, sacred freedom, dance
and song to smuggle out.
                    The Delphi in him
urging him on, four times over by choice
a fugitive, barefoot through mud and rocks,
the flinty cold of more than half of Europe,
living on wild berries, the fulfillments,
raptures of the hunted:
                    in certain seasons
thrilling as ever the pain inside his bones.

Cast on this shore, the language of his youth
much like the rubble of the world he fled
and foreign phrases, stubborn on the tongue
as new terrains to aging sinews, futile

also, once again he tries through speech
the market-place and the arena use
to reach the latest young.
                                The magic works:

II

Exchange goes on, a subtle flow-
ing in and out of lilac breath,
exchange a dialog as though
someone were feeding, feeding
were thus fed:
                        the well-assorted
voices in his voice that rage
with lilac, grape, the open sea,
as it rolls up, the secrets
of one's life, lovely on its crest:

and morning like that flambeau
grating fury first ignited,
morning flung from crag to crag,
grown lucid in the wrangling wills:

bow-twang and lyre-, speedy passage
to the spires of snow-glimmer-
ing Parnassus and the summits
over it of stars, the dark
a shadow of what avid thought?

and still the light upon his words
as day, plunging, gladly lingers
in the wings of sportive birds,
the lady's owl-eyed, leafy gazing.

III

Wherever you go you will be a polis.

But where is Athens, once that city
in the clouds? Now nameless rubble

most of it, many times nameless—
lilac, asphodel and poppy
famous through its cracks and stubble—

ruins in the wind of what
mad whirling, monstrous with delight,
rushed by, a passion beyond purpose,
hope, too fierce for shape, Athens
pebble shiny in its reeling,

pillars fallen as their gods,
then raised again to fall again
for Vandals, Turks, Venetians, Franks,
the Romans, its own restless will
and a hundred moods of tameless time:

like an enormous cicada shell
of some now-far catastrophe,
the crumbling Parthenon.
       Strange
that as one stands in it—
       a dancing
in and out with civil light,
those airy massive girls, that eagle
lit on steadfast wind—
      and gazes
through its broken skeleton
the town below should look so whole,
so radiant.
    And here, the dusk
wine-spilt on the hills, the stars
as they leaned on these pillars once,
near for the centuries ago
they first began, in twinkling airs
repeat their haunting names again.

IV

A pebble in the mouth of one
whose tongue rolls round, a pebble sounding plumbless fathoms, fames of time.

And it rolls round, metropolis
and temples, traffic rumbling beauty,
clouds resounding, tides:
                              the wine-
skin foot, released, leaps forth,
capricious as a satyr, dulcet
drunkenness where, mouth to mouth
gods and men combining,
                              Athens—
rooted as the strophes of the stars
within the wine-sack of the grape,
like dawn swept down on us through leaf
and flake, the lilac's sudden rippling—
purls through lips and shaping hands.

Airs for Caliban

A COMPETITION

Martyr complex? Not on your life.
Just that on such a peevish Sunday
one has to find diversion somehow.
Soon, before you know, you're so
absorbed by what you're doing,
much like that moony one stuck
on himself in a river, everything
else seems wishy-washy, trivial.

Exactly then, precisely as he's
entered you, the god decides
to be resentful, raging, sputters
to himself: "If he thinks he can
get away with it, be entertained,
be slaked as I am, with the gifts
and fruits of his own nature,
why he's crazy. I'll teach him

a thing or two!" He challenges.
The sack I am begins to shake;
the sweetnesses my own fermenting
makes, the honey-pungent airs,
grow clammy, cloud, base vinegar
the taste of me.
        O what he wants
is plain enough: to beat me
at his game, pluck me from myself
by scaring me (whose ecstasy?)
out of my skin.
        And thereupon,
when I, my veins in sight, am one
great aching wound, a naked man,
hung out on some old tree to dry,

he fills me with his favorite foam-
y bubblings and drinks as his own
piping wills.
           Though to be so
roused as he then was and sing
(in anger, true) so well makes me
wonder whether the wine I was
and that he must have tippled on,
exceeding me, did not inspire him.

CLOTHES MAKETH THE MAN

(to be read aloud awkwardly)

How hard it is, we say,
how very hard. Clearly no one can say
these cluttered lines and make them
stride or make them stay. No actress
in the land—the best have tried—
can find a pattern or a rhythm
in such befuddled monologue.
                                        Concede,
I say, it is a role to test the mettle
of a Bernhardt who, wigged, without a leg
and in a ragged voice could—so they say—
strike any rock-like audience to tears,
this with only the alphabet.
                                        Maybe,
you say, maybe. But then the alphabet
by Racine, no less.
                                And I am depressed.
Ah me, I am depressed to think how we,
with many more outspoken words, submit
to mutterings and silence, only answer
fitting our despair.
                                How hard it is,
we say, how very hard, that we should find
ourselves stuck in such muck.
                                        Oh well,
I say, maybe when we haven't understood
each other long enough, it will prove
stubborn stuff that we can carve.

Already Goya knew the sharp rebuff
of nakedness. With nothing between
he almost wrung his naked Maja's neck,

as though he'd stuck the head of one girl,
a much beloved, on the body of another
(for less aesthetic uses, say), and they
would not set, not in the daring solvent
of his paints.
   His Maja draped was
a far different matter. I say! I never
thought I'd prefer a dressed girl to one
undressed. Even for me, I see, it's later
than I guessed.
   So let's go home to bed,
Renée, and dress and dress and dress.

IN ANY CASE

The Whorfian Hypothesis—
             "Language
by its structure influences thought
and our perception of, responses
to, the world"—
        is true.
            As you,
your guidebook idioms buzzed round
my head, go on and on this hour,
with your accent so pronounced,
the time beween us and our trip-
to-be fast slipping by,
             jostled
on our bed as on some narrow,
prickly wagon-lit, I, sniffing
smoke, confused with rakish cries
of countries we are twirling through,
wearily complain,
           "If only you
were practicing the dialect windy
sycamores and crickets use."
             But then
those acrobatic vocables begin
to work
       (this language knows, if you
and I do not, the things it's after:
spices, wines are mellowed in,
and body follows scents the mind
evokes):
         the autumn night, our stuffy
room begin to be—no doubt in moon-
lit, easygoing rain and laughter—
less than a block or two from April's
Luxembourg.

Surprised that though
I catch no more than demisemiquavers
and understand, in any case,
French even less, I turn to you,
entirely convinced?
　　　　　O you may say
that by my overall sense of structure
I am much impressed.

STUDYING FRENCH

some thirty years too late
(the rhythms do declare themselves,
the glints, through clumsy clouds,
through stiff-as-frozen clods,
the flowers in their revery),

I, who love our English words
and loll in them against
the several terror and the cold
like any little furry animal
grown cocky in his hole, begin

to understand past supple words
the language you and I grope
toward and, reaching, wander in
among the periods of doubt,
those long ice-numbing nights

when deserts seem to travel
us at their own stately speed
and fury like a moony beast,
a speechless, glacier-capable,
goes poking its rough tongue,

so searching, into the crevices,
the weaknesses, of everything.
For one long given over
to another tongue this French
is much too hard. It makes me

doubt myself, my easy hold
on everything, and everything.
I who debonairly strolled
(I rallied them, I twitted them
with double talk) among my words

like one among his animals,
once wild, but now their strength,
their rippling colors, blazoned
on him, can smell once more
the threatening smolder, smoke

behind them, open fields so fine
for pouncings and hot blood,
the void in flower we go out
to meet, hand clutched in hand,
as it ransacks us for its tutoyer.

RUINS FOR THESE TIMES

I

To hell with holy relics,
sniffing like some mangy dog
after old, dead scents (saints?),
those that went this way before
and went. More shambling about
in abandoned, clammy churches
and I abjure all religion,
even my own!
            It's much too late
to heft a Yorick skull and, ear
to it as to a surf-mad shell,
hold forth foul breath to breath
on man's estate.
            What's more
I, plundered, plundering,
out of these forty odd bumbling
years have heaped up spoils
with spells compelling
enough, my own:
            a father
who keeps coming apart however
I try to patch him together
again. Old age too much for him,
the slowly being picked to pieces
as a boy with a fly, he hopped
a spunky horse and left
change gaping in the dust.
            Mother
too who would not watch herself
turn into blind and stinking
stone, took things into her own
hands, finished a rotten job
with a rush.

II

But lest I seem
too personal, let me cite
the grand, efficient, ruin-making
fashion of our time.
This earth,
a star, brave and portly once,
now like a chimney belches
filthiest smoke, fallout
of roasting human meat the air
we breathe;
the ember-eyes
of millions I have never seen
(yet relatives the more for this,
stand-ins for the role
I missed by sheerest accident)
flare up within my dream's
effective dark.
O let Odysseus,
Hamlet, and their sparkling
ilk grope after; here's
a midnight ought to satisfy
the genius in them.

III

Let them.
What's the mess of Europe,
late or antique, great or antic,
to the likes of me?
Pottering
about in my own cluttered memory,
I turn up, still in full career,
my grandfather, muscles sprung
from dragging packs through miles
of factories:
a grandmother
who bore, conscripted lifelong

to the total war of hunger
and a strange new world,
three families on her back
and then outwore them all
as she outwore her ailments,
one enough to fell a warrior:

that friend whose breath shaped
songs desperately debonair
out of our snarling dog-eat-dog
accomplishments.

IV

               There too
I poke out bits, still standing,
from my wrecks, begun in fervor,
aspiration, joy:
               those passages
through which the morning strode,
enlightened in its retinue,
choke on the plaster falling,
raspy stenches, refuse of lives
trapped in them.
               Is the building
lust for ruin so strong in those gone
before that I and mine are nothing
but a story added, foundation
for new ruins?
               The prospect
that seemed the way to heaven
glimmers mainly with the promise
of a final storm, a monument
of glittering bones to gratify
most dogged fates.
               Our own.

AN OPENING FIELD

for Stefan Hirsch

To mind and not to mind,
to be exposed, open
(like a barn, its rafters
and its walls collapsing,
and the summer, prying
through the gaps, rolls
round among unbinding mows,
its tumbled light so sifted
in the strawy rifts), to mind
and not to mind,

                    ignoring death,
yet for, awaiting it like one
long played on that the airs
recall his sense of being,
open so that wasps may enter,
throbbing like a central nerve,
wasps and the many moods
the summer, simmering
from one bed as it wakens,
then the next, is given to . . .

you see your painter friend,
once buoyant to the world,
now broken by the flogging
blows his gentleness
exposed him to: through love,
no less than the world's
indifference, these strike.
And as he, dragged along
by his dog on their daily
latenoon walk, draws near,

you ask, "Where are you
going?" At first he fails
to notice you, looks about
as though a voice he cannot
see were calling him. Then,
like one returned from far
away, he peers at you.
"Geh kotzen," he replies.
"But first I've got to find
someone with shiny shoes."

"That's dangerous," you warn.
"Add to the mess already here,
and we'll be over our heads
in it." He nods. Then gazing
up through the cleft
in the trees to the field
beyond: "How fine it is!
No matter what we do
or say, it still goes on
the way it has to, lovely."

The field, light full,
as though the sun delayed,
among the border-sloping
trees and in and out
the solitary trees, has
slowly mellowed, a meeting—
as from its own accumulating—
of mild and generous,
intensely calm (a master's
fitting) glances.
                    And he,
who has minded too much
and, overwhelmed—memories
at him troubling still—
stumbles into things,
simplicity a light upon

his face, breaks into smiles:
that bottom purity, blowing
ever more strongly, greets
the world from which it's come.

SONG TOWARD MORNING

Deny the innocence
of need? With more than twenty
years gone by, still as one
in bonds and wingless yearns
to fly, cram sky in earth,
he strains to say how much

she means, means far
beyond herself. Earth's dark
around, he clutches one object,
then the next, grips cloudy air,
and nothing works, not words
the wise fell dumb before

that seemed to perch
on mountain tops, on tipsy
crests the sea keeps tossing
in hurrahs, and strident stars,
nor music even, not the one
impatient of the masks

of things and poised
in air, turned on itself,
a bodied nakedness. Not that
or this, pervasive helplessness.
But when the dark seems most
complete, he stumbles on

that scene in which
a woman looks with body-
focused wonder at some glory
just beyond the painting's edge.
And as she looks, an angel,
knelt, wings quivered

(molting one, aflutter
as if heaven's wind blew
in it still, but then no worse
for miracles than the hairy wen
upon her chin, her winning,
easy loss of balance)

as in outmost flight,
is pondering her as though
through what she understands
and what in small and fragile
flesh befriends she staggers
him, a first time seeing

in another and more
taking light what had ever
been his wish, his dream,
his chief insight. Just so she
might have stood, recovering
from that gust, the air

already settled on
the white and battering
attack, its wake still wild
in her. The moon is anchored
so and, like these beings
rooted in their loves,

most as its search-
ing gaze, the light it sheds
and thereby speeds inside—
as does her mouth upon
its words, her eyes reaching along their glance—

attains its charm
far out beyond itself
and moves the sea and earth

into the dance it moves among:
it seems amazed with every
muted, kindred image

it is not, yet helps
to be, as though all pluck
their lot and substance
from its hand and are, as it
alights, its homecome morning
song, its lucky site.

FOR HOPKINS AT OXFORD

Towery city still, tolled in its towers,
rooks recalled by crumbled kings and martyrs.
These, dumbfounded, with the gargoyles glare
at grey descendants, peddling by, who swirl—
where paths had idled for the cowslips twirling—
back and forth from pre-fab, shop, and pub.

Air fumes. The Thames, carefree minstrel once
of sail-quipt argosies and ruffled queens,
stammers a muddy tale of small-fry fishermen.
Flocked the streets with bleak and yokel face,
a kin to those of Scotus' time, itinerant
after purse and lust, their learning's scent.

Still, as in your words, the gypsy-player
seasons hawking your wares, this world endures.
In unexpected courts, by leafy servitors
with swans that grace whatever impulse passes,
the earth, a sweet brown study, and the air
your love made vivid after him live on.

For you have shown what worthy thing it is
to furnish grief with all the rage and nettles
of this life and yet not yield your pity
or your love that like a maddened, aged king,
so crowned, last manliness achieved, grief sing,
the wind, the dust, its daughters, echoing.

THE VISIT

I

Paris, Winter

To paint without a model,
shun all visits so that what one wants
to do cannot be interrupted or distracted,
as though the many strokes were someone
drawing near, the putting down of a land-
scape that cannot be till it composes
itself like a woman combing her hair,
touching up her face, arranging her shawl.

And then the lover, straining
at himself as at the distance that
intervenes, appears. The evening begins . . .

the evening began early, often shortly
after morning (which, plunged sputtering
down the well, bucketed back again
in a clatter of pots, the cries and smells
mixed in the courtyard, burst against
the walleyed window), in our scabby room
nearby the Luxembourg . . .
                              the rain
would soon be lowering its boulevards
and fountains, upstart there to launch toy
boats with furry boys and grandpapas
marauding golden coasts of smudgy Africa

till noon, bustling up beside the hedges,
in its shadows light upon the couples,
restive as a clutch of pigeons, flapping
out a crackly sky, full speech, around them . . .

you and I feel bare; our English dangling
like any bottomless pitcher over there
or what one might try to say to a world
absolutely deaf (and yet, we think,
if only we talk loud enough . . .), we huddle
in our room.
                Still this so-wintry page
looks English back at me as much as French.
And while you shiver in the crumpled bed,
I try by rubbing words to rummage out
a fire, at least one smoky morning ember,
a mumbling bird.
                I have, you know, learned
how to paint without a model, how to risk
no visits, many times O long ago.

II

                Cambridge, Mass., Summer
To paint without a model,
shun all visits so that what one wants
to do cannot be interrupted or distracted,
as though the many strokes were someone
drawing near . . .
             and so the evening begins . . .

the evening began early, often shortly
after . . . no, I know that will not do
(what's Paris to the backwood likes of me
from tribes remembered best for kitchen-middens),
not that setting, not its tense, not all
the cries and smells.
              Though they a moment
might have bellied out that someone's breath
as flotsam helps to ruffle up a flood,
they were, especially to French as skilled
as mine
          (and anyway perched now in Cambridge,
Mass., for all their clapped-together, clapboard

churches, as much my state as the Puritans':
the garbage, spewing out of cans, in steamy
stench an Indian prince, haloed by flies,
remarking it no more, no less, than if
in Paradise, droning their own mass),

too self-engrossed.
      The someone drawing near,
under cover of this clatter, by the cast,
the grandpapas, the boated, puffy boys,
already in their play halfway to Africa

(somewhere, it is true, along that well,
in one room or another—shutters fastened,
still a deeply searching smell seeps out—
beside the bureau and a foundering bed,
the chairs, awry as with a gale, one guise
of him appears and, eyes glimmering
among the tears, blood spit, is happily,
absorbedly at work),
      reflected in that
rain, each fountain spouting him, the maples
too, the shady glints the couples quarry
in the bushes,
     slipt away.

      (Outside,
a hullabaloo: machinery, shouts. I listen,
drop my spluttering pen, dash out.

Before my door a main, clogged with debris
yesterday's hurricane swept in, has burst.
Watching the pleated water row the street,
as though at last the sea had found some
one small vent, I think of all the showers,
noon and evening thirsts, the flapping sail-
loud sheets and shirts on lines, washing
down the drain.
     By now the giant crane—
a man with a white flower at one ear,

a skinny kid beside him, its quick brain—
has eaten out a crater in the street,
and four six-footers, heads around my knee,
with cries and thigh-high boots are sloshing
through the glossy mud.
                              A flurry of kids
like flotsam tossed up on the little flood
eddies shrilly at the curb.
                              One tries
his homemade boat along the gutter;
it throbs at once to water's impulse
and its own, then merrily bobs as though
days out on the high seas.)

                              Again that someone
slips away.
                    And I, like a cave dweller,
squatting in that old familiar smell,
mixed with the dump's fuming a sniff away,
his damp flint hunting fire, company
he loves so well
                    (the hulking, aerial
shapes he daubs on crooked stones, like him
who lay long months in clammy dark, heaven
flaking in his eyes),
                    behind façades
of odors, outcries, mad towns crashing by,
you fiddling in a corner, more and more
at home in Bach,
                    I huddle in our room,
waiting for the words, struck countless times,
to open, let the genie, burnt-match-black
and hot with incense, treasure, out: let me,
Eden-deep and sweeping-past-desire, in.

III

                    New York, Spring
To paint without a model,

shun all visits so that what one wants
to do cannot be interrupted or distracted,
as though the many strokes were someone
drawing near . . .
                              and so the evening begins.
Once more the stage is set, the properties
of night, so thick with wall in wall in wall
and bending to the page the stars are muffled
like the reassuring common faces
of the day.
                    Yet there to be completely
open, nothing on my hands, no help,
no pre-established passwords, nothing but
my innermost, most desperate need,
                                        the some-
one drawing near, deftly as a woman
touching up her eyes with brush-strokes
that apprentice to their purpose light,
my look, the rain's legerdemain
                              (I feel,
I hear the flowers stirring, birds behind
already coming, combing out in flocks
fat, multifoliate summers),
                              open so
that in these lines what, taunting, passes
daily haunts and shapes, exultant
through the cast-off nimbus of a name,
nakedly appear.
                    "Terror is not French,"
Rimbaud said. Nor is it rustlings, siren,
savage, of the bush, a bug's argot,
the strange, lost mutterings of tribes
long dead.
                    Yet who shall say by way of beds,
the mirror with its making mouths (nacreous
cries submerged in it, the flesh still greedy
in the far-receding waves, moon giddy
as it dips in sherry, eyes), what does
get said.

Three apples, lustrous in this bowl,
plumped out as a speech: that cocky maple
at the window, blathering its head off,
full of country matters still: the rain,
running in and out its own Spenserian
exercises, blueprint of a wordy summer
crowding one small bush,

       these, as I paint
without a model, risk no visits, express
themselves, and so consummately, so plainly
what they are, no record can be made,
nor need it be.

     But what about the whispers
from next door, the voices burrowed in me
also, murmurings too close to hear?

   "A marching on the floor above,
   below, those in cellars, attics,
   boarded-over, mumble only
   hot, taut glances as they wait,
   the days one dark, for who knows
   whom, the sky lit up with friends
   and kindred, echoing through sleep,
   their hearts the thud of shovels,
   earth, slapped into newdug holes."
           Night,
once freshest air, heaven itself come, candid,
down to breathe with us, has turned into
a sealed-in cave, one wall in wall in wall,
a grave sodded with graves, till even sky
seems underground.

     And sitting in this room,
one of many thousands like a Chinese box,
rather than these roses, apoplectic
as with your heart's blood, the walls' pale idiot
staring, havoc you desire, shearing
through the rooms.

     Inside this city, gypsy
city going up, collapsing, like tents

pitched in a desert, how can these words,
burrowed into, save?
                    Do we not brush
the roaches basking there, the lordly rats,
the corpses heaped, their bloody whimperings,
as in these walls?
                    Listen. Familiar names,
the breathing hived, lost tribes, sound up again.
The ungainsayable honey-breath of spring,
your silvered glance, as cool and penetrating
as the rain, bursts through the dust and lights
on me, stirring birds and flowers, towing
multifoliate, fat summers.
                    Faces,
haloed in their touching innocence,
the reassuring common faces of the day,
whatever sweat and weariness, repeat
through crow's-feet indefatigable hope,
the child they keep, the child they keep on
being, shining more and more for every crease,
so bless this life, the thing I try to say.

I, for a time at least, by these as by
the hungry words invoking them past speech,
am spared that final visit, its one cap-
ping stroke.

IV

Annandale-on-Hudson, Autumn

(the voices burrowed in me . . .)

Anywhere they happen:
in this learned light now, ripening
through autumn, as though the mellowing
earth had finally imprinted itself,
a gloss, upon the quiet air,

as on the straw-in-amber-
bright pine-needles, matting the little

footbridge, anywhere they start up,
transported from a many-placed,
a many-timed remoteness,

breathing out a young
Egyptian morning, like the Nile brimmed
for its glittering rigs that seem
to bear it, there, surprising
as a passage in an old,

familiar book, frequently
reviewed, yet deeper now. Unfolding in my flesh, incognito, they travel,
waiting for me, feted in a look,
a phrase—this butterfly,

an eyelid long forgotten:
sunbeams, cleaving the dovetailed
trees, the laughter of my desert-wander-
ing friend and, far behind him,
in him, those who dared

the Red Sea and a desert
also for their dreaming of a land
sweet milk and honey—speeding, waiting,
to speed me farther on my course,
sufficiently looked after.

V

                       "But that's,"
she said, "more farfetched yet. There is,
it seems, no stopping you. The scene
you sketched, electric in its promises
and threats, you haven't used. Instead you
introduce another scene, another, still another,
topping that.
               Whatever happened to the woman
shivering in bed? Was she the one who

worshipped at her mirror first? Or to that lover,
smart in terror and delight? The evening too
they might have reveled in?
                              Gone, all gone,
and scarcely touched upon. And you impressed
with palming off a lot of garbled copies,
each more preposterous than the last, copies
of a lost original; no doubt
a fake at that!"
                  Don't be so sure. That woman
may be you, you the more she changes, changing,
always more the same, much like the face
one finally comes to.
                       Out of all that squalor
piled on squalor—no ancient cities built
on cities better—I would show that scene
and in its very shiftings,
                            show it fresh
as a new flower, proved, improved perhaps,
in each transplanting, unbetrayed by thought
or what it has been through, just like a mirror,
polished by the world of pictures flitting
in it, bountiful for its own sake alone.

The scene, well traveled, is unfolding, crisp
as ever, crystal parks and dapper, swift-
paced boulevards, the traffic civil, movements
of a woman, weaving through our steel
and glass, mirror-fluent, rain . . .

    and then the lover, straining
    at himself as at the distance that
    intervenes, appears . . .